Animal Habitats

Table of Contents

by Emma Rose

Getting Started

No matter where in the world you go, you can find animals. Animals make their homes in all kinds of places, or **habitats**. A habitat may be hot or cold. It may be wet or dry. A habitat may be dark or sunny.

Habitats must have what animals need to survive—food, water, shelter, and room to grow. Not all animals live in the same kinds of habitats. Let's explore four different habitats.

In the Sea

Most of Earth is under the sea. The sea is a wet and salty habitat. It is the home of big and little animals, such as whales, sharks, and shrimp.

Why is the sea a good home for certain animals? The animals can find food all through the sea, from the top of the water to the seafloor. The animals have room to hide, move, and grow.

This fish is a blue tang. Its home is in the warm, shallow waters of a **reef**. Small animals called *coral* make up the reef. Plants and animals grow on the reef. Sea animals use the reef for homes or food.

Deep in the sea, it is cold and dark. Big fish like flounder and cod swim here. They look for small fish to eat. Some animals, such as this hermit crab, live on the seafloor. They hide in the rocks and sand.

In the Woodland

A **woodland** has a lot of trees and other plants. Trees are plants that make good homes and food for animals. In summer the woodland is a cool, shady habitat.

In the woods, dead plants on the ground can be good homes, too. If you were to lift up a log, what might you see? Animals! Insects, snakes, and mice can find good homes in logs.

This shrew lives in the northern woods. It eats insects. In the fall, the shrew stores food in the tunnels it digs. Why? In winter many insects die, making it hard for the shrew to find food. Then the shrew eats the food it stored.

Moose make their home in the cold woods of the far north. In winter, they dig in the snow to find plants to eat. In summer, a moose will stand in a lake and chew on plants growing on the bottom of the lake.

All kinds of birds live in the woodlands, too. Many of them build nests in the trees. Owls and hawks hunt mice. This habitat is a busy place!

In the Rain Forest

In the **rain forest**, rain falls on the leaves of the tall trees. The leaves are so close together, they form a green "roof" that shades this hot, wet forest. The rain drips down the leaves and tree trunks to the ground.

The treetops are called the *canopy*. Some animals, such as monkeys, like to stay up in the canopy during the daytime and whenever it rains.

canopy

understory

forest floor

The part of the rain forest below the canopy is called the *understory*. The understory is home to smaller animals, such as snakes and bats. On the ground, or *forest floor*, it is dark and hot. A lot of ants live here!

Tigers or other big cats may roam through the rain forest at night. They hunt for food. In the heat of the day, tigers rest. A big cat may even climb a tree to find a cool spot for a nap.

In the Arctic

The **Arctic** is a land of ice and snow. This habitat is home to many animals, like the polar bear. In the short summer season, the sun never sets here. Plants must grow fast before the land grows very dark and cold. Animals must eat while they can.

Winter is a long season in the Arctic. It is cold and dark all the time. To survive the winter, animals must be able to stay warm and find food.

This walrus has a lot of fat called *blubber*. The blubber helps to keep the walrus's body warm. A walrus can use its tusks like spoons. It can dig clams out of shallow Arctic waters to eat.

An arctic fox's fur turns white in the winter. It turns white so that the fox can hide in the snow and not be seen.

Look outside! What animals live in the habitat where you live?

Index